Sigrid Schöpe

Translated by Coralie Hughes

Training and Riding with Cones and Poles

Over 40 Engaging Exercises to Improve Your
Horse's Focus and Response to the Aids, While
Sharpening Your Timing and Accuracy

TRAFALGAR SQUARE
North Pomfret, Vermont

First published in the English language in 2015 by
Trafalgar Square Books
North Pomfret, Vermont 05053

Originally published in the German language as *Reittraining mit Stangen und Pylonen* by Franckh-Kosmos Verlags, Stuttgart

Trafalgar Square Books encourages the use of approved safety helmets in all equestrian sports and activities.

Library of Congress Control Number: 2014958970

All photographs by Horst Streitferdt/Kosmos
Illustrations by Cornelia Koller

Cover design by RM Didier
Typefaces: Din, Didot

Printed in China

10 9 8 7 6 5 4 3

Getting Started

Training Exercises with Poles

Training Exercises with Cones

Ending on a Good Note

Key

Next to each exercise you will find a "dot" symbol, which indicates the level of difficulty:

●●●   Easy Exercise
●●●   Moderate Exercise
●●●   Difficult Exercise

This key should help you choose your focus during each lesson, as well as expand your training program over time.

Getting Started

Enjoyment of the training process—that's what rider and horse should always maintain, even when they take riding and being ridden seriously. Many common training exercises don't help rider and horse progress; they are boring and destroy motivation. In this book, I would like to show you easy ways to bring new energy to training and riding your horse.

MAKING RIDING FUN

Everyone knows the "usual" arena figures, such as serpentines, voltes, and circles. It is generally understood that they gymnasticize the horse, train the rider's seat, and refine correct aids. But what do you do when your circle looks like an egg, the horse isn't bending evenly, or he's dragging his feet so lifelessly through the sand that you would rather just get off?

In the pages ahead I will give you a wealth of ideas that can bring variety and energy back to your training program. Using simple "props," such as ground poles, cones, or even buckets and barrels, you can increase your own concentration and that of your horse, while making ridden exercises more interesting and challenging.

In this playful way the horse is effectively trained and his coordination refined, while the seat of the rider becomes more secure and her aids more precise. Both partners develop an improved perception of where their bodies are in space and how they move.

It is not complicated to do these exercises. I give you different variations that fall in three categories: Easy, Moderate, and Difficult. You don't have to read this book all the way through. The exercises don't build on each other in the classical sense. Based on your knowledge of yourself and your horse, you can choose what you want to work on at any given time. Is your horse stiff and not bending well? Or do you want to improve connection and

contact? Choose the exercise that best fits you and your horse during a particular lesson. Don't start with the most difficult exercise. When easier exercises are achieved, praise your horse generously, and only then increase the challenge. Your goal is to keep your horse motivated.

All the exercises in this book improve the horse's concentration and strengthen the relationship you have with him.

Earning the Horse's Trust ●●●

Trust on both sides is an important prerequisite for any work with a horse. Consequently, our first exercise is to introduce the horse to the equipment in the arena or riding area. Depending on how comfortable your horse already is with cones, poles, or buckets and barrels (should you use them), this exercise can take very little or a lot of time. Be patient when it is necessary and praise your horse when he stays calm.

WHAT YOU NEED

Cones: Colorful traffic cones are available from many do-it-yourself supply or hardware stores. When you buy new cones, make sure they are sturdy. You can also use empty buckets (remove the handles!) in place of cones. Many of the exercises in this book require four to six cones.

Poles: It doesn't matter if the ground poles you have are colorful or natural, or made out of plastic or wood. You need up to six ground poles, all of the same length.

For some of the exercises, you can also use swimming noodles in place of poles. But be careful: Noodles are very light and can be blown by the wind, which can potentially frighten your horse.

Cavalletti: Several exercises use cavalletti—raised poles—which demand more attention from the horse because he must lift his legs higher.

Let your horse quietly look at and sniff the objects you plan to use in training exercises. If he lowers his head in the process—perfect! Lowering the head helps him to relax.

Praise your horse a lot when you work with him. This builds trust and shows the horse that he is doing well.

HOW TO DO IT

Distribute the objects you will be working with around your riding area. Regardless whether you've arranged poles, cones, buckets, or barrels, lead your horse to each individual obstacle. This is especially important when your horse isn't very comfortable with certain objects. Many horses have a problem with brightly colored items. Let the horse quietly walk over the poles, around the cones, and sniff everything. Praise him when he stays calm and quiet. If he is frightened, circle him quietly, and approach the "dangerous" object again. Should an object prove difficult, you can try placing treats on or near it. When schooling with items the horse is fearful of, don't stand in front of him in case he suddenly jumps or scoots forward—instead, stay next to his neck and shoulder.

As soon as your horse is calm around all the objects, you can mount and warm up.

Tip

To maintain your horse's concentration, give him a break from the exercises every 15 to 20 minutes. If your horse is still young or inexperienced, he may tire even faster.

Don't try too many things at once during a lesson. Select in advance just one or two exercises you want to practice. As soon as you notice the horse is losing interest, stop and give your horse a break.

I keep a training journal and note which exercises I have done with what horses and how it went. This journal reminds me what we have done so I remember what to work on while still being sure not to always practice the same thing.

Warming Up ●●●

You must include time for you and your horse to warm up every time you ride. Ride at a walk on a long rein a few times around the arena, just as you would before any riding lesson or training session. You horse should move fluidly forward and stretch his neck and back. If you are stiff, it is also a good idea for you to move your own body the first several times around. When horse and rider are both supple and focused, it is time to begin.

When your horse softly chews the bit during warm-up, it is a sign of a good work atmosphere.

HOW TO DO IT

Even before getting on your horse you can stretch and warm him up, using groundwork. Let your horse walk a few rounds on the longe line or in the round pen, and then trot him a little. Stretching and bending in the neck and back are good opportunities to loosen up the horse.

Once you get on, supple your horse and slowly develop his focus, first by riding around the arena, then by doing large circles or serpentines with large arcs.

Make sure you are sitting in a supple and relaxed way on your horse. At the walk, you can do little loosening up exercises, assuming your horse won't get nervous with you moving around in the saddle. For example, turn your upper body to the right and left, reaching down to grab your toes. Lean forward to scratch your horse behind the ears and lean back to scratch him on the croup. Circle your arms. Feel the movement of the horse and go with him. Your ability to communicate with the horse is more precise, the more flexible and sensitive you feel, and the better able you are to react to his movements.

When your horse is supple and focused at the walk, ride a few times around at the trot. Change the length of the reins: ride with a long rein, then take the reins up and make contact with the horse's mouth. A short canter is fine in the warm-up when the horse is ready. Notice if he chews the bit peacefully.

1 The rider should also loosen up before training begins, such as leaning forward to scratch the horse between the ears.
2 Movements from side to side, as done here, improve coordination.
3 Reach back and touch the horse's hind end. You will be more supple and flexible in the saddle afterward.

Riding with a Plan ●●●

When you've planned your ride well, you have a head start. Before your session, choose two or three exercises you want to try. Arrange the poles or cones in advance and make sure the distances between obstacles "fit" your horse's stride, size, and experience. You will exude confidence when you have a plan and know exactly what you want to do. Your horse will then follow you trustingly wherever you go!

You are the leader. Your horse will happily follow if you know exactly where you are going.

WHAT IT LOOKS LIKE

During your warm-up, practice riding with a plan by riding near the poles and cones you've set up. The straight and bending lines you ride should be big, however—avoid tight turns.

Think ahead about where you want to ride and at what gait. Don't attack your horse with your aids. Fix on the point you want to ride to without stiffening up. Keep an eye out for the general area and other riders, if you are schooling with others. Your head, shoulders, and body will follow your eyes, and this will also direct your horse. Try it.

HOW TO DO IT

The big advantage to working with poles and cones is that they provide fixed points on which to focus, helping you orient yourself in the arena and making it easier to ride a line. A volte—a very small circle of 6, 8, or 10 meters in diameter—is rounder when the rider concentrates on a cone in the middle. Turns are easier when the space is well defined by poles or cones.

Place a cone in the middle of the ring (at "X" in a dressage arena). Ride around the arena on the rail, turning toward the cone at the center of one of the short sides (at "A" or "C" in a dressage arena) and ride directly toward it. Right before you ask the horse to turn, look at your goal! Your "plan" and focus on the cone will cause you to hold the reins more softly and your head and upper body straight. You will also find that your horse moves in a straight line to the cone.

You can also ride on a circle around the cone. Look intently in the direction toward your goal of an evenly bending line, keeping the cone as your center point in the corner of your eye, and turn your body slightly. The horse will follow your movement. Always be clear where you are riding to and at what speed. Don't be sloppy with any exercise, no matter how easy. Follow a picture in your head that tells you "this is how it should look." A clear goal helps you to ride more precisely, even when it doesn't work right away.

1 Keep your eye on your goal. It is important that you have a plan and a mental picture of how the exercise should look.
2 Cones or poles are optical aids, which help you and your horse follow the desired line. Use these aids in your training!

Tip

Is your horse sluggish and lacking impulsion? Look ahead in the distance, and he might suddenly pick up his tempo. Avoid staring at the ground. A hanging head negatively affects your whole seat.

Training Exercises with Poles

Why is pole work good for you and your horse? In general, the exercises I provide, whether they use one or several poles, look quite simple. However, they require a high level of concentration from rider and horse. The rider must give the aids precisely and sensitively. The horse must pay attention and follow the rider's instructions step by step. Mistakes are immediately obvious because the horse knocks or steps on the poles.

FEELING AND TRUSTING

Poles "fence the horse in." That means they help the horse try to stay within the boundaries of a pathway or a pole square, for example. At first, though, when the exercise is difficult or your horse can't bend well, he will try to evade a movement and probably step over the poles.

Depending on the exercise, you may be working on impulsion or collection of the horse; on rhythm, suppleness, or straightness; on lateral movements or correct turns. It is a question of balance, the horse listening to the signals of the rider and responding precisely, and the rider feeling the horse's movements and *also* responding precisely. Some horses have a difficult time with ground poles

because they have a hard time seeing them or knowing where they are. For example, during a leg-yield, the pole might be under the horse's belly, so he must depend on the rider to guide him over it. This strengthens trust between them as partners.

When you incorporate pole exercises in your training, your horse must consciously place his feet step by step. Carelessly shuffling through the exercise or fidgeting around without focus doesn't work. Anxious horses often become calmer with pole work, and lazy horses are motivated by small successes, participating more enthusiastically and moving more briskly forward after the exercise. Stiff horses are gymnasticized without

becoming bored. The rider trains her ability to "feel" and refines how she gives the aids: Which leg must the horse move next? Where are the hindquarters in relation to the poles? How much pressure do I need to use to get the reaction I want? Pole exercises help in almost *all* areas of riding—and they improve both horse and rider.

Step by Step over a Pole ●●●

Patience required! An exercise that can look very easy at first, but which can actually be quite difficult, is to walk with the horse step by step, leg by leg, over a pole. Regardless of whether the horse is led from the ground or ridden, he should only put one leg over the pole, then stand still, then bring the second leg over the pole, and stand still again, and so on. Most horses try to take at least two steps—one leg after the other—over the pole.

Here I am saying, "Come to me!"

WHAT IT LOOKS LIKE

Place a pole on the ground, and beginning first on the ground as shown here and progress to working from the saddle, ask your horse to step, one leg at a time, over the pole. He should do each leg only at your command and consciously wait attentively for your signal, pausing in between steps. He should also lift his legs carefully to clear the obstacle.

"Stop!" The horse should halt as soon as he has put one leg over the pole. If the horse steps with his second leg before you can stop him, send him back a step as a correction, and try again.

1 We have paused with one leg over the pole. Time for the next step!

2 Praise! My horses know the sign: When I crouch down beside them, that means, "You have done well!"

HOW TO DO IT

It is not so simple to lead or ride a horse step by step over a pole. The horse must clearly understand the commands to halt and move forward. It is also important that your horse concentrates on you. Don't practice this when there is commotion in or around the arena.

If you walk or ride straight to the middle of the pole and stop as soon as your horse has put the first hoof over the pole, it is usually already too late. By then, the horse has already moved his second foot. This is where you will see why it is better to train this exercise first from the ground: You have more control when leading over the pole because you can watch the horse's feet.

As soon as the horse has taken the first step over the pole, stop him immediately. You can do that by turning to face him or by putting your hand up to stop him (without pulling on the halter or rope). Praise your horse and let him stand still and relaxed for a few moments before asking him to continue on. Pull slightly on the rope to ask him to take another step forward, and watch carefully for his reaction. If your horse grows restless or inattentive, lead him around the arena for a bit, and then try again.

Once you have mastered the exercise from the ground, try it from the saddle. Remember to not pull on the reins! When the horse goes too far and steps with the second leg over the pole, it is your fault for not giving the aid to stop at the right time. Exit the exercise and start over from the beginning, as this is preferable to confusing your horse by moving him back and forth.

Leg-Yield Down a Pole ●●●

You can practice rhythmic and straight leg-yields **forward-and-sideways with a single ground pole.** This exercise requires concentration and coordination. The horse learns to understand and correctly follow forward-and-sideways-driving aids. Since a pole is under his belly as he moves forward, he must trust his rider. Once the basic leg-yield down the pole is done well, the exercise can be varied, as you'll see in the pages ahead. Make sure you do it in both directions.

WHAT IT LOOKS LIKE

The simplest way to practice a leg-yield down a single ground pole is to align the horse's front end in front of the pole and use the pole as you might the wall or rail of an arena. The pole serves as an optical guideline to orient horse and rider.

It is more difficult to do this exercise with the pole between the horse's front and hind legs, under his belly, as shown in the pictures. If this makes your horse anxious, begin the exercise from the ground.

Don't let your horse leg-yield all the way along the pole right away. Begin with just two or three steps, and increase from there when your horse understands what he is supposed to do.

Approach the ground pole so that the pole will be under the belly of the horse, with his front legs on one side and his hind legs on the other. When you first try this, begin in the middle of the pole, rather than the end, which is more difficult.

HOW TO DO IT

When trying this exercise from the ground, watch your horse's feet. They should stay on either side of the pole. The forward-sideways movement down the pole should be in a straight line. If not, correct the horse immediately, but don't confuse him by pushing him back and forth. It is better to exit the exercise, walk in a small circle, and begin again in the middle of the pole. Stand at the side of the horse, by his girthline, and ask him to move forward and over, with his front end slightly leading his hind end and both sets of legs crossing. If your horse wants to move too much forward, hold briefly on the halter or apply a little backward pressure, and then send him forward-and-sideways again.

When riding this exercise, shift your weight in the saddle slightly in the direction of the movement. The horse is flexed away from the direction of movement. Your outside leg (*outside* the flexion—so the side that faces the direction you are moving) is applied a little behind the girth while your inside leg (*inside* the flexion) drives the horse forward-and-sideways at the girth. Hold the outside rein against the horse's neck, and maintain a light contact on the inside rein to maintain flexion. If your horse steps forward or backward and is no longer straddling the pole, ride a large circle and begin again.

Make sure that fluidity and rhythm are maintained. The horse's neck should not be overflexed.

With correct weight and leg aids from the saddle, your horse will cross his legs while going forward-and-sideways. Pay attention to your seat!

Don't ask your horse to leg-yield down the whole length of the pole right away! Increase the distance gradually.

Leg-Yield Down and Back ●●○

When horse and rider have mastered the leg-yield down the single ground pole, it should look soft and fluid. The horse should step over in a regular and supple way without rushing; the pole always stays under the horse's belly, with his front and hind legs straddling it. Then it is time to try a new variation so it doesn't get boring: Get a second pole!

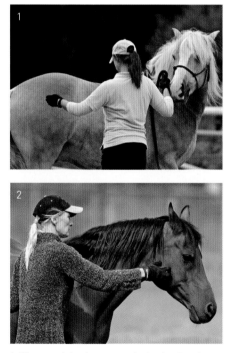

1 When practicing the turn-on-the-forehand on the ground, ask the horse to move his hind end over by applying pressure toward his croup.

2 For a turn-on-the-haunches, ask the horse to move his front end by applying pressure toward the head.

WHAT IT LOOKS LIKE

Set two ground poles about 6½ to 8 feet (2 to 2½ meters) apart, so there is a "path" between them. As in Exercise 5 (see p. 12), the horse should leg-yield forward-and-sideways, straddling the first pole. You want to go more sideways than forward now, so the horse's front end will not lead to the same degree it did in that exercise. At the end, turn and straddle the second pole and leg-yield back down it.

At the turn from one pole to the next, your horse can make a simple turn, or you can try a turn-on-the-haunches or the forehand. This exercise is best practiced from the ground in the beginning. The way you start the exercise depends on the kind of turn you plan to make.

Leg-Yield with a Turn-on-the-Haunches
In this variation, at the beginning of the exercise, the hindquarters of the horse are in the "path" between the poles, and the forehand is outside. Ask the horse to leg-yield to the end of the first pole. Then do a turn-on-the-haunches with the forelegs moving around the hind legs, which almost remain in place. The horse should then be standing, facing the opposite direction, with his front legs in the correct position outside the second pole and his hindquarters still in the "path." You might have to adjust the poles to accommodate the size of the horse.

Horse and rider prepare for the leg-yield down the pole. The rider looks in the direction of travel with her weight over her inside (the side closest to the direction she's traveling) seat bone. Her outside leg (furthest from the direction of travel) is positioned a little back behind the girth.

The "Learning Effect"

To avoid the horse swaying back and forth during the leg-yield, the rider must concentrate on maintaining a precise seat and giving precise aids. With practice, the horse trusts his rider more and gains balance. This exercise, which requires a lot of concentration on the part of both horse and rider, improves not only the horse's response to the leg but also great timing for both. This is the desired "learning effect." You can control how well the exercise goes: Does your stirrup always stay directly above the ground pole? When it does, then the horse is moving straight!

Leg-Yield with a Turn-on-the-Forehand
To make this turn, change the position of the horse so that you begin the exercise with his forehand in the "path" between the two poles, and the hind end on the outside. Leg-yield down to the end of the first pole, ask the horse to perform a turn-on-the-forehand where his hind end moves around his forehand, which basically stays in the same spot. After the turn, the horse should be straddling the second pole, again with his forehand in the "path" and his hindquarters on the outside. Then the horse can leg-yield along the second pole to the end.

HOW TO DO IT

When practicing this exercise from the ground, pay attention to your position relative to the horse. If the forehand is supposed to move (turn-on-the-haunches), stand near the shoulder. If you want to influence the hindquarters (turn-on-the-forehand), stand closer to the croup.

To ride a turn-on-the-forehand, flex the horse with the inside rein (so if you are asking the horse to move his hindquarters to the left, this is your right rein), and give driving impulses with the inside (right) leg at the girth. The outside rein and leg control the horse's steps as the hind legs move around the front end, which remains basically in place.

To ride a turn-on-the-hindquarters, "show the horse the way" with the inside rein (the horse is flexed in the direction you want him to turn) by gently moving your hand sideways. At the same time, push a little forward with the inside leg (inside the turn) at the girth. The "guarding" outside leg drives the horse to step his front legs around while his hind end remains in place.

The "L" ●●○

You can also practice the leg-yield with two ground poles set up in an "L" shape. Now, as in the last exercise (p. 14), you may want to move more sideways than forward down the poles—almost a sidepass. The hard part is getting around the corner. When the horse has his front legs positioned "inside" the "L," you can move around the corner with a turn-on-the-forehand. When the hindquarters are "inside" the "L," you can move around the corner with a turn-on-the-haunches.

The horse is concentrating on the exercise, paying close attention to his rider and her aids, as he is slightly flexed away from the direction of travel and crossing his legs. Note that while his front end is still leading, he is moving more sideways than in the photo on the previous page.

When positioned as this horse and rider are, with the horse's front legs "inside" the "L," begin a turn-on-the-forehand right before the corner. You may look down for a moment in order to orient yourself.

WHAT IT LOOKS LIKE

Starting at either the center of one pole or at the end, apply the aids for the leg-yield. Plan ahead for your turn as the horse moves forward-and-sideways to the corner of the "L." As mentioned, when the front legs of the horse are inside the "L," you must move the hind legs around the front end at the corner, and vice versa if the hind legs are in the "L."

If your horse has mastered the turn-on-the-forehand, begin with that. If he is better at turn-on-the-haunches, plan to start there. Poles make an added challenge for the horse, so be patient. After the corner and turn, again ask the horse to move forward-and-sideways until you reach the end of the second pole. Since the horse moves off the same leg through the whole exercise, his flexion stays the same.

With a turn-on-the-forehand in the "L," the horse's front legs should remain in the corner as the hind end moves around the "outside" of the obstacle. The poles should help limit the movement of the horse's front end.

After the turn-on-the-forehand, continue down the ground pole in a correct leg-yield. Praise your horse when you reach the end.

HOW TO DO IT

Riding the turn-on-the-forehand in the "L" moves the horse's hindquarters about 90 degrees around his forehand. Flex the horse with the inside rein (away from the direction of movement—so if you're traveling toward the left, your *right* rein) so that you can see his eye. Weight your inside (right) seat bone. Your inside leg drives from a little behind the girth while the outside (left) leg maintains a "guarding" position to prevent the hindquarters from moving around the forehand too quickly or imprecisely. The outside rein limits the horse's movement of the front end and prevents his shoulder from popping out. Look in the direction you are turning the haunches.

When riding a turn-on-the-haunches in the "L," the front legs move about 90 degrees around the hindquarters, which remain in about the same place in the corner of the obstacle. There will be a change of flexion from the leg-yield (the horse is flexed *away* from the direction of movement) to the turn-on-the-haunches, when the rein on the side of the direction you are traveling must "show the horse the way." If you are asking the horse to do a turn-on-the-haunches to the right, for example, weight your right seat bone. The right rein introduces the turn, and your right leg is at the girth, encouraging forward movement. Your outside (left) leg causes the horse's front legs to step around the turn. The outside rein limits the bend, but yields enough so that the horse can move in the direction of the movement. Note that whenever attempting the leg-yield with turn exercises, it is better for the horse to step forward than to step backward in the case of resistance.

The Double "L" •••

You can ride through the Double "L"—a "channel" created from two pairs of ground poles placed in a parallel "L" formation—forward and backward. The 90-degree corner usually is not a problem when moving forward; however, the difficulty shouldn't be underestimated when backing up. Horse and rider must both concentrate on every step around the corner to avoid stepping outside of the "L" poles on either side.

WHAT IT LOOKS LIKE

Walk forward through the Double "L" created by the two sets of poles and halt at the end. After a brief pause, ask the horse to back through the same space, step by step. Pay attention to each step and maintain a straight line—avoid the horse hitting or stepping over the poles. If he does, quietly move forward out of the Double "L" and begin the exercise again.

Just before your horse reaches the corner, pause briefly to give him a chance to focus on the turn while he's moving backward. The horse should step slowly with his hind legs around the corner so his body is aligned and he can back the rest of the way out of the Double "L."

1-2 Moving forward through the Double "L" is no problem for most horses—you can do it at the trot to increase the challenge.

HOW TO DO IT

When trying the exercise from the ground, walk the horse forward through the Double "L," ask him to halt at the end, then lay your hand on the horse's nose to ask him to back up, or send him backward with a hand signal. Just before the turn, you may need to step outside the Double "L" to guide your horse in the correct direction—but don't let your horse! If his hindquarters need to move to the left, move his head gently to the right, and vice versa. Ask slowly and thoughtfully for your horse must think the exercise through and sort out his legs!

When riding, the more difficult part is backing up straight and then through the corner. It is important to place your aids correctly. If the horse's hindquarters must move to the left around the corner, place your right leg a little back behind the girth while limiting his front end with your reins. Go slowly. Give yourself and your horse time. Give the aids step by step with your leg. Maintain a light contact with the reins. Never pull the horse backward with the reins!

After the turn, straighten your horse before asking him to back the rest of the way through the Double "L." Don't forget to praise him!

For some horses this is a demanding exercise. When done well, take a break or end the training session.

1 Avoid rushing the horse as you ask him to move backward. It is better to let him think a little bit in the corner.

2 The diagonal pair of legs should step backward at the same time. To lighten the load on the horse's back and encourage backward movement, bend a little forward, as shown here.

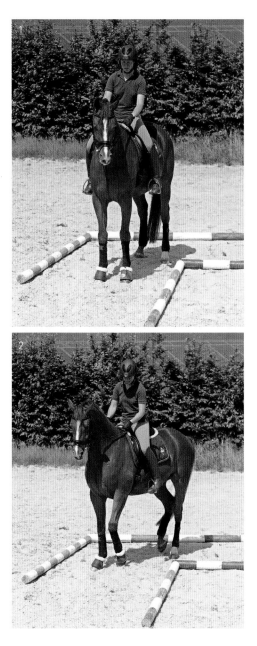

Double "L" Combination ●●●

In this exercise you will combine the turn-on-the-forehand and the turn-on-the-haunches with the leg-yield. As before, have a plan: Think about what you are doing in advance so that you won't have to stop in the middle of the exercise in order to determine where and how you must go. This combination requires a lot of concentration from you and your horse, not only for the individual "pieces," but for the whole exercise. At the end of the exercise, let your horse relax on a long rein.

WHAT IT LOOKS LIKE

Begin at one end of the Double "L" with the hindquarters of the horse "outside" and his front feet "inside" the Double "L" (see diagram). Perform the leg-yield along the ground pole until you reach the corner. Then make a turn-on-the-forehand 90 degrees or so until your horse is positioned with his front and hind feet on either side of the second pole. Again, leg-yield. At the end of the second ground pole, ride forward several steps so your horse now has his forehand "outside" the opposite pole and his hind end "inside" the Double "L." Leg-yield to the corner. After another turn-on-the-forehand, leg-yield again along the pole until you exit the Double "L."

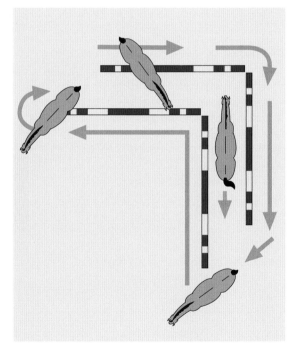

At the end of the fourth ground pole, do a 90-degree turn-on-the-haunches so your horse's hindquarters are positioned in the middle and parallel to the ground poles on either side. Ask the horse to back through the Double "L" to finish the exercise (see p. 18).

Staying focused and accurate through the Double "L" requires thoughtful preparation: Where am I going? How do I have to sit? And...

... what are my leg aids?

HOW TO DO IT

When first practicing this exercise from the ground you must pay attention to your body position. To ask your horse for the forward-and-sideways, leg-yield, stand at his belly. To move the forehand, step to his shoulder and neck. To move the hind end, stand at his flank. If your horse responds to hand signals, you only need to point to the shoulder or flank to get your horse to move the fore- or hindquarters over, or tap him there lightly.

From the saddle, you must combine the aids for the leg-yield (p. 12), the turn-on-the-forehand, and the turn-on-the-haunches.

When performing the turn-on-the-forehand to the left as in the illustrated example on p. 17, weight your inside (in this case, the right) seat bone and drive with the inside (right) leg behind the girth while your outside (left) leg holds a "guarding" position and prevents the hindquarters from moving too quickly. Your outside (left) rein restricts the horse enough to keep his

forehand in place and prevent the shoulders from falling out.

In the turn-on-the-haunches to the right, keep your weight to the inside (right) with your inside (right) leg lightly driving at the girth. Your outside (left) leg asks the horse to step around with pressure just behind the girth. The inside rein initiates the turn, while the outside rein limits the horse's movement and keeps him stepping around rather than just forward. Remember to "give" now and then with the outside rein so the horse can bend in the direction of the turn.

The "Learning Effect"

The turn-on-the-forehand schools the horse's response to the sideways-driving aids. The turn-on-the-haunches is not only a good exercise to develop concentration, it also increases collection since the horse shifts his center of gravity back as he steps around his hind legs.

Riding over Ground Poles ●●●

Even simple pole exercises **require impulsion and increase activity
in the horse's hindquarters. For example, just riding over several
poles in a row teaches the horse to lift his legs actively and move
in a regular rhythm. The rider becomes more supple and secure in
her seat.**

WHAT IT LOOKS LIKE

Begin with three or four ground poles. The
distance between the poles depends on the
size of your horse, his length of stride, and
also the gait in which you are working. A standard place to begin is with the poles approxi-
mately 2½ feet (.8 meters) apart at the walk
and 4¼ feet (1.3 meters) apart at the trot. You
can increase the number of poles later.

To begin, ride with a long rein at the walk
over the poles. (If the poles are too close
together or too far apart for your horse, you

will notice that he moves irregularly and hits
the poles. Adjust the distances as necessary
and take care that he doesn't hurt himself!)

If your horse is unsure or evades sideways, trying to avoid the ground poles, lay
them out along a fence line to start with. This
way, you only have to worry about one side.

When you and your horse are comfortable doing the exercise at the walk in both
directions, ride it at the trot after adjusting the
distance between the poles. The horse should
step over the poles fluidly in a regular rhythm.

Here you can see a "staggered" setup: The distance
between the red-and-white poles is greater and appropriate for the trot stride of this horse (see sidebar on p. 23).

After the last pole, "give" the reins and let your horse
stretch forward and downward.

1 Go over the poles with your hands slightly forward so your horse can look to see where he is going. Note that your upper arms should stay near your body.

2 This exercise can be done with a partner when both horses have a similar length of stride. This can be fun for the riders and the horses.

HOW TO DO IT

When first leading the horse over the poles from the ground, move briskly alongside your horse and let the lead rope hang loose. Your horse should move freely forward, striding fluidly over the poles, and you shouldn't have to pull him! If he is sluggish or refuses, it is better to drive him from behind with a flick or tap of a whip than to drag on his head.

When doing this exercise from the saddle, pay attention to the tempo and rhythm of the horse's gaits—they should be regular. As you ride to the first pole at the walk or trot, give your hands forward to allow the horse to look where he is stepping. Maintain a consistent, elastic connection with the horse's mouth. Stay in balance with your horse. You will notice that the "swing" of his back increases when he goes over the poles. After the poles, reward the horse with a stretch, then pick the reins up, ride around the arena, and try it again.

Variation: Staggered Poles

You can also stagger the poles about 1½ feet (1/2 meter) to the left or right (see left photo on p. 22). This presents new possibilities: You can ride to the left or right, meaning over every pole, or every other pole. One side is set at the standard trot stride, and the other side increases the distance between poles so that not every trot step crosses a pole, causing the horse to have to concentrate.

Serpentines between Poles ●●●

Serpentines can be practiced between ground poles. **The poles pro-**
vide a boundary that makes traveling the path of the serpentine much
easier, as you will find. Lay out the number of poles according to the
number of serpentine half-circles you want to ride. Serpentines are
effective tools to supple and gymnasticize the horse.

WHAT IT LOOKS LIKE

Place four to six poles so they are spaced
evenly apart. Don't put the poles too close to
the edge of the arena or work area because
your horse needs enough room to make the
serpentine turns on each side of the poles.
Begin by riding through the "path" created
between the first two poles on one end, turn
at the end of the path in an arc, and then ride
through the path created by the second and
third poles, and so on. If you want to make a
bigger arc, you can skip a path and vary the
size of the serpentine. Start out with only a
few poles and increase the number (and thus

the number of serpentine half-circles) when
all goes well.

HOW TO DO IT

When trying this exercise from the ground,
stand at the end of the first ground pole and
ask your horse to walk around you in a half-
circle. Then lead him down the "path" created
between the first and second ground poles.

If your horse doesn't yet know how to do
a half-circle around you using hand signals
and body language, you can support the
horse's hindquarters with the light touch of
a whip.

When riding this exercise, maintain a light contact on the reins so the horse can stretch forward as he walks. Make sure he doesn't go around the poles stiffly. The goal of the exercise is to achieve a supple and consistent bend. It is better to ride a larger serpentine turn than one that is too small. You don't need to turn into the very next path between poles if it is too challenging for your horse to bend that much. Note that every horse has one side through which he bends more easily than the other. Start your serpentine so you bend in the easier direction. This will make the exercise more achievable and positive for you and your horse.

Be precise in your seat: Turn your upper body and shoulders in the direction of movement and remember that you must make your horse straight again after every bending half-circle.

When attempting this exercise at the trot, it is easier for the horse if you go slowly. Adjust your seat in enough time to help the horse begin the next turn in the serpentine.

In contrast to the Four-Leaf Clover (see p. 70) or the Figure-Eight with Zigzag Poles (see p. 40), you have time in this exercise to guide the horse in the right direction. Riding serpentines between poles is a good way to prepare for more difficult exercises.

1 Watch that your horse stays straight when between the poles and doesn't start bending into a turn until he reaches the end of a set of poles.

2 Ride straight until it is time to ride into the bend as the serpentine heads for the next set of poles. Maintain a correct seat. Your horse should not run through the shoulder, as he is in Photo 2, but should bend through his entire body.

3 Your horse should travel through the poles straight...and you should sit straight!

4 In Photo 4, you can see that the horse is bending correctly (compare to Photo 2). Don't forget to praise your horse at the end of the exercise.

Simple Turn in the "Funnel" •••

Ground poles offer a wide variety of exercises **that increase concentration and coordination in both horse and rider. You can practice tight turns in the "funnel," which is a contained space created with five poles. Similar exercises are sometimes seen in trail classes.**

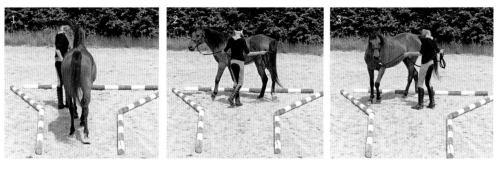

1-4 Lead your horse into the funnel, keeping him in the center of the first path created by the two parallel poles. At the top of the funnel, turn him around and head back in the opposite direction. Don't start your initial turn too late!

WHAT IT LOOKS LIKE

Make a path out of two poles laid parallel to each other, about 5 to 6½ feet (1½ to 2 meters) apart. Then place two more poles at one end, each slightly angled to the outside. "Close" the funnel shape in with a final pole placed from the end of one angled pole to the other.

The shape and size of your funnel will need to be adjusted to accommodate the size of your horse. The "top" of the funnel (where you turn) can be smaller for small horses and ponies. It will need to be wider for large breeds so these horses can comfortably turn around without stepping outside the pole boundary.

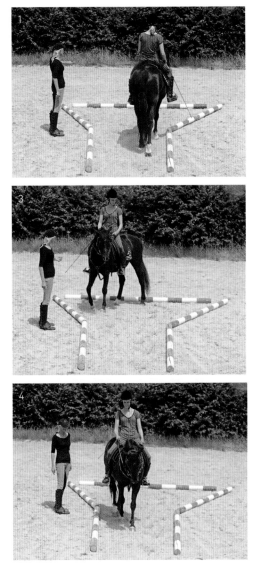

1-4 Ride straight into the funnel, and when you reach the "top," concentrate on helping the horse trace the arc of a half-circle with his body. Use the whole funnel for your turn, riding well into the corners created by the poles.

HOW TO DO IT

When practicing from the ground and leading your horse through the funnel, pay attention to your position. Don't hold the horse too short. Walk straight into the funnel. At the "top" where the funnel widens, ask your horse to walk in a half-circle around you, as if you were longeing him. Shift your position from in front of to the middle of the horse (see Photos 2 and 3 on p. 26) to ask your horse to bend around you. Then walk beside your horse straight out of the funnel the same way you entered.

When riding this exercise enter the funnel straight. At the end of the parallel poles, where the funnel widens, begin the turn (a half-volte). So, when turning to your left: Apply inside (left) rein to initiate the turn, shift your weight to the inside, and move your outside (right) leg a little back, just behind the girth. Your inside leg is active in the turn to encourage forward movement. Complete the half-turn in this way, and then go straight between the parallel poles and exit the funnel.

Make sure you turn your upper body correctly in the direction of the turn and don't collapse at your hip. In addition, the horse should bend evenly through his body and not just his neck.

Turn-on-the-Forehand in the "Funnel" ●●●

To increase the difficulty of the funnel exercise you learned on
p. 26, try a turn-on-the-forehand (or a turn-on-the-haunches—see p. 15) in
the funnel. This helps you gain a feel for where the horse's legs are beneath
you. Your aids determine whether the horse can make the turn in the funnel without stepping outside the boundary created by the poles. When first
attempting this exercise, you may look down briefly to see where you are.

WHAT IT LOOKS LIKE

As in the original exercise, ride straight into the funnel,
centered between the set of parallel poles. Plan where
you wil halt and begin your turn. The horse's forehand
should be in the center of the "top" of the funnel so his
hindquarters can turn around his forehand while staying inside the poles.

Move carefully, step by step. Don't be overanxious
or erratic with your aids. Praise your horse when the
exercise goes well.

After completing the turn-on-the-forehand ride
straight out of the funnel.

HOW TO DO IT

Once you've reached your chosen spot in the center of
the "top" of the funnel, prepare your horse for doing
a turn-on-the-forehand to the right or to the left. If,
for example, you are asking your horse to step toward
the right as shown in the photos, your horse should
be slightly flexed to the left with your inside (left) rein
as your outside (right) rein prevents too much forward
movement. Your inside leg is applied at the girth and
drives the horse's hindquarters step by step around his
forehand as your outside leg supports him.

If your horse tries to step forward, take a little
more contact on the reins. The outside (right) rein, in
particular, and your outside leg, control the movement.

1 Romeo is standing too far forward in the
funnel. . .

2 . . . so as you can see, he has a difficult time
completing the turn-on-the-forehand within the
pole boundary. In this case it is better to stop the
exercise, exit the funnel, and start over again.

Turn-on-the-Haunches in the "Funnel" ●●●

As we learned on p. 15, with the turn-on-the-haunches, **the horse's forehand moves around the hind legs, as they remain almost in place. It is important that the horse takes small controlled steps with his front legs rather than simply throwing himself around. Again, make sure that the horse has enough space when you halt at the "top" of the funnel to perform the movement without hitting the poles or stepping outside the boundary.**

WHAT IT LOOKS LIKE

Begin as you did in the previous exercise and ride forward and straight between the two parallel poles until the horse is standing with his hindquarters in the center of the "top" of the funnel. Guide the horse's forehand step by step around the hindquarters. Ideally, the hind legs should step almost in place. Don't hurry. When you have completed the turn, ride straight out of the funnel, and praise your horse.

HOW TO DO IT

When beginning on the ground, walk briskly with your horse into the funnel. Halt with his hind end in the center of the "top" of the funnel, and position yourself next to the horse's shoulder on either side so that you can ask the horse to move his forehand around his hind end. Walk with the horse's forehand in a half-circle around the haunches.

From the saddle, when performing a turn-on-the-haunches to the left, enter the funnel and travel straight to the halt. Shift your weight for the turn on the haunches to the inside (left), position your inside leg at the girth with your outside (right) leg a little behind the girth. The inside (left) rein initiates the bend, the outside rein controls the horse's forward movement. Give a little on the outside rein so the horse can turn toward the left. Make sure you aren't pulling the horse around by the inside rein. He only needs to be slightly flexed in the direction of the turn.

Teach your horse to move away from pressure from the ground. Stand between the horse's head and shoulder, facing his neck. Place one hand on his jaw and the other hand on his shoulder. Push lightly.

Volte over "T" Poles ●●○

The *volte* is a small circle with a diameter of 6, 8, or 10 meters. You can ride voltes of varying size over a "T" made with ground poles. The secret to this exercise is to ride half the volte on the flat ground and the other half over the poles, requiring the horse to pay attention to when he must step over the poles. This develops focus and concentration.

WHAT IT LOOKS LIKE

Place two ground poles one after the other in a straight line. In the middle, where the two poles meet, lay a third pole perpendicular to the other two, forming a "T" with a short "leg" and a long "top." The "T" should be arranged in an area where you and your horse have room to ride around it. Begin the exercise by riding a large volte that crosses over all three poles. Practice voltes both to the left and to the right. Pay attention to your path of travel so the beginning point and ending point of the volte are at the same spot.

1 As you ride a volte flex the horse to the inside of the circle and look at the point where all the poles intersect.

2 Your outside rein guides the horse and your inside rein asks him to position his body on the bending track of the volte.

3 Stay soft in the hand—do not pull the horse into the volte with the inside rein.

HOW TO DO IT

Leading the horse, walk around the poles, then a bending line that crosses over all three poles. When you walk alongside the horse, the circle can be big, and is a good place to start. You can also stand at the intersection point of the three poles and ask the horse to walk in a circle around you, as if you are longeing him. Take care that your horse crosses the middle of each pole if possible.

In the saddle, ride in a walk circle around the "T" without going over the poles. Then, still at a walk, ask your horse to step over the individual poles without hitting them with his hooves.

Start your first volte on the "open" side of the "T" of poles (the side without the perpendicular third pole) and make the diameter as big as you can while being able to cross the end of each pole. If the horse shies away or avoids a pole, come back and try again.

Once your horse understands what you are asking, shrink the volte, but don't overdo it. Ride a few voltes of different sizes, then let your horse have a break.

Then, reverse direction and start the exercise again, beginning by going around the poles. Progress to different size voltes at walk and trot. Don't forget to praise your horse!

Tip

The size of the volte you ride—larger or smaller—depends on your horse's level of training and his size. In the pictures you can see that Romeo can make very small voltes, partly because he is relatively small. The volte should be ridden larger with bigger horses because of their longer length of stride. Note that the bending line of the volte should remain the same around the "open" side of the "T."

A correct seat and position are important when riding this exercise. Whether making a volte to the left or right, use your inside rein (inside the circle) to position your horse on the bending line, and weight your inside seat bone. Bring your inside shoulder a little back and your outside shoulder a little forward. Encourage your horse forward with your inside leg at the girth. The outside leg "guards" just behind the girth, preventing the hindquarters from swinging out.

Leg-Yield with the "T" ●●●

In addition to training voltes and circles, **you can use the "T" configuration of poles to work on riding the leg-yield. There are all kinds of possible
combinations.**

The leg-yield as you will use it here is best practiced with one pole first
(see p. 12). Then, try this exercise, and be creative with the "T." Change up
between circles, half-voltes, and leg-yields over and across the poles.

Start with a volte around the "T" of poles. If you have done
the last exercise (see p. 30), your horse might already be
comfortable with this.

When adding the leg-yield, decide in advance which pole you
want to halt over before asking the horse to begin moving
forward-and-sideways.

With his rider in position to request a leg-yield, Romeo moves smoothly down the pole to the right. He is bent slightly away from the direction of travel, and his forehand leads slightly.

Make your aids as soft as possible. You want your horse to "straddle" the pole, and not step forward or backward over it as you leg-yield.

WHAT IT LOOKS LIKE

Start in the last third of the perpendicular ground pole (the "leg" in your "T"), riding forward until your horse's front feet are on one side of the pole, and his hind feet are on the other—straddling it. Ask your horse to leg-yield down the pole to the top of the "T." Then try the same movement after performing a volte over all three poles.

HOW TO DO IT

When beginning from the ground, stand next to the horse's shoulder and use hand signals or pressure on his jaw and flank to ask him to move away from you and down the pole. Control his head with the lead so the horse doesn't step forward over the poles with his hind feet.

While riding, it is important to use your weight correctly in this exercise. In the leg-yield, the horse is flexed away from the direction of movement but his body should be almost straight—his forehand will slightly lead his hind end, depending on the amount of forward and the amount of sideways you are requesting.

Begin the movement with a volte, and when you reach the perpendicular pole, straddle it and practice a few sideways steps, then go forward again. Repeat the exercise, slowly increasing the number of steps down the pole in the leg-yield until your horse willingly goes the whole length, crossing his legs smoothly. If your horse breaks away or gets resistant, don't punish him. Just circle, and start over.

Over the Corner with Zigzag Poles ●●●

With ground poles set up in a zigzag pattern, you have multiple exercise possibilities. You can lead or ride the horse straight over the poles, or you can incorporate serpentines, voltes, figure eights—whatever you can think of!

Here I describe my favorite exercises with zigzag poles. See which ones you and your horse like best.

This is how a wide zigzag setup should look.

Here you see a narrow zigzag, for comparison. This is appropriate for Romeo because he is small. Note that he is carefully watching where he places his feet.

WHAT IT LOOKS LIKE

Place four poles on the ground in a zigzag pattern as shown in the photos. Make the zigzag wider or narrower as suits the size of your horse.

Lead or ride your horse in a straight line over the poles. Vary the exercise by riding toward the middle of the poles, or more toward the side with two closed "points" or the side with two open ends.

Encourage your horse to step fluidly and evenly over the poles. Ideally, he should not rub or knock the poles with his feet.

HOW TO DO IT

When leading the horse from the ground, walk beside him, either close at his side (you walk over the poles, too) or at a slight distance (you walk outside the poles). Either way, the lead rope should hang loose—don't pull on the horse. You set the speed and direction, not the other way around!

When riding, "give" with the reins, a good hands-breadth forward, so your horse can see the poles well while you still maintain a light contact. Ride in a straight line. Your horse must pay attention to the changing distances between the poles. Sit lightly in the saddle and don't drive too much with your seat. When you try the exercise at the trot, go slowly and stay in sync with your horse, unloading his back, by moving your upper body a little forward.

You can add a lot of variety to your schooling session with zigzag poles. Near the "points" where the poles are closer together, your horse must take shorter steps. Near the open sides, your horse must find the correct number of steps that fit between the poles. Look at how carefully Rodenjo places his feet in the photos!

Serpentines with Zigzag Poles ●●○

With good longitudinal (from nose to tail) bend, **ride your horse in a shallow serpentine over the zigzag poles. He must watch where he places his feet as you ask him to change bend from left to right and vice versa. This exercise demands concentration and coordination in the horse, activates the hindquarters, and enhances body awareness.**

WHAT IT LOOKS LIKE

Ride the horse in a shallow serpentine over the zigzag poles with correct flexion and bend. Between the "points" where two poles join, switch your horse's bend to the new direction. Movement should be fluid and supple and the contact light. A well-trained horse can quickly learn to be ridden through this exercise, guided only with changes to how the rider distributes her weight.

HOW TO DO IT

Go through the exercise from the ground first, paying as much attention to the horse's bend in the serpentine as you will when riding him. It is better to walk with your horse with correct bend in larger half-circles than in smaller unbalanced curves. Correct bend is necessary for the exercise to have a gymnasticizing effect.

1 The inside rein (inside the turn—here, the left) asks the horse for inside bend, and the outside rein "gives" a bit to allow it.

2 Keep control of the horse's outside shoulder—in this photo, the right one.

3 Romeo is ready for the next bending line of the serpentine, arcing right toward the pole.

4 The horse shouldn't overbend through the neck like Romeo is here.

5 Look where you are going. The body follows the eyes.

6 End with praise for a job well done!

Once you are in the saddle, you will find your horse bends more easily to one side than the other. Begin your serpentine with this side.

Initiate the bend by flexing the horse with the inside (inside the curve) rein. The outside rein must "give" about the same amount that the inside rein asks for so the horse can bend through his neck. Your inside leg drives at the girth and your outside leg is back slightly behind the girth in a "guarding" position to control the haunches.

As you cross each pole and go through the "open" areas of the zigzag, change the weight distribution of your seat and begin the turn in the next direction. The difficulty of this exercise is in the repositioning of the horse at the right moment. Watch your seat aids. They must be used as clearly and quickly as your leg aids. The serpentine should be ridden over the poles in a fluid right-left-right-left combination of arcs.

Voltes over Zigzag Poles ●●○

Voltes are perfectly round small circles—at least in theory. Every honest rider admits it is not so easy to ride a volte that is even all the way round. Practicing voltes can get boring for you and your horse, and it can help to use zigzag poles to keep sessions interesting. Voltes with zigzag poles are fun, have high gymnastic value, and activate the horse's inside hind leg—that is, if you do the exercise correctly from the beginning.

WHAT IT LOOKS LIKE

On the side of the zigzag poles with two "points" where poles touch, select one of the "points," and ride the horse in a large volte around the point. Then ride straight over the two angled poles in the middle, followed by another volte around the second "point."

Both voltes should be the same size and maintain the "point" where two poles meet as the center.

Ride the exercise with a change of direction so you practice voltes both to the right and the left. This ensures your horse is gymnasticized on both sides.

Experiment with the size of the angles in your zigzag to best enable your horse to circle evenly with consistent bend.

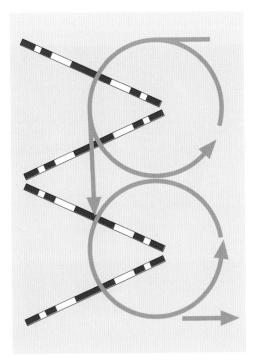

HOW TO DO IT

Try this first from the ground, paying as much attention to the distances between obstacles and the size of your volte as you do from the saddle. This is often forgotten when doing groundwork!

Walk the pattern of both voltes along with your horse. Then, stand at one of the "points" and ask your horse to walk around you in a small or large volte, as if longeing him. Switch to the other "point," and send your horse out onto another volte around you.

When riding, be precise with your aids, as instructed in earlier exercises. Weight, leg, and rein aids must be given at the right time and in the right combination. Just as when you are riding voltes without the addition of ground poles, position your horse for the bending line with the inside rein (inside the bend). This "positioning" is a very small movement at the horse's poll. The outside rein softens a little to allow the flexion.

Your horse should bend evenly all the way around the volte, without his haunches or shoulders falling out or in. It can help to remind your horse to stay straight by giving him a tap on his inside shoulder with the whip.

Don't hold the reins too tight or your horse will only bend in his neck, rather than longitudinally through his body. The bend must be through the whole horse. Bend him around your inside leg, which lies softly against his belly. Your outside leg supports him. Your body should stay straight in the saddle.

1 Remember, as already mentioned, when working with ground poles, it is important to give your horse enough freedom of his head so he can see the poles. Keep in mind that horses have a different field of sight than we do.
2 Don't "lock" your hands, which can happen when you are riding multiple voltes in a series. Maintain a soft, feeling connection with your horse's mouth. The exercise should feel smooth and fluid.

Figure Eight with Zigzag Poles ●●●

The most demanding exercise with zigzag poles is to lead or ride the horse over them in figure eight patterns. This is difficult because the zigzag poles lie in varying distances—the poles meet at a "point" at one end with a much wider "open" side at the other end. This variable provides a good learning experience for your horse.

WHAT IT LOOKS LIKE

From the ground, stand at one of the "points" on the two-"point" side of the pole zigzag and longe your horse over the poles and around you, using an extra-long lead rope. Show him the direction with one hand (called the leading hand), and hold the excess rope in the other hand. To change direction for a figure

eight, at first, stop the horse, switch your leading hand, and show the horse the way over the poles in the new direction as you move to the second "point" of the zigzag. He should turn in front of you and continue on a circle. With a little practice you will be able to do this change of hand without stopping the horse.

Here you can clearly see how I show my horse the direction with my leading hand.

When you practice this exercise from the saddle, don't ride the figure eights too tight; instead make large, generous bending lines.

After working over the zigzag poles, ride around the arena on a long rein so your horse can stretch and relax.

Ride the circles of the figure eights one after the other in the following combination: circle left, circle right, circle left, completing two figure eights that encircle all three "points" of the zigzag poles.

Start this exercise at the walk, as the pattern is not simple and the poles provide a real challenge for the horse. Later, you can try it at the trot, but not until the horse can complete the exercise slowly without hitting the poles. Your aids must be given softly and smoothly or the exercise is worthless.

HOW TO DO IT

When leading the horse from the ground, you must take care that you move with your horse at the right time to the next "point." This transition is challenging for you and takes some practice.

Riding the exercise requires coordination. I recommend mastering the previous exercise (see p. 24) before attempting the figure eights with zigzag poles. As mentioned, the difficulty lies in the uneven spacing of the poles due to the zigzag configuration. You have to adjust your horse's stride at the right time and pay attention to his footfalls—and he must remain focused, as well—or he will stumble against the poles.

Begin in a quiet walk and indicate the bend required with your weight and leg aids. When you feel like the exercise is going well for you and your horse, try it at the trot—note that you will likely need to adjust the pole distances to accommodate your horse's stride.

Remember: This exercise is deceptively simple and actually requires a high degree of concentration from your horse. So, don't train too long over the poles! Give your horse a break after a job well done.

The Fan ●●●

Riding over poles laid out like a fan (see photo) develops suppleness and rhythm in the horse. For this exercise you need five poles. As you arrange them on the ground, it is important to pay attention to the correct distances. If you have a small horse, the poles need to be closer together, while a large horse requires they are arranged farther from one another. You can then ride a circle or volte (see p. 30) over the poles in either walk or trot.

WHAT IT LOOKS LIKE

Place the ground poles in a fan formation, with one end of each pole close to the others at a central "point" and the other ends "opening" and spread away from each other. Start with three poles and work up to five. At the walk, the distance beween the middle of one pole to the middle of the next should be between 1¼ and 2½ feet (40 to 80 centimeters), depending on the stride length of your horse. At the trot it is more like 3 to 4 feet (90 to 120 centimeters).

Walk with your horse over the middle of the poles, in hand. Then try it at the trot, again in hand. In this way you can adjust as necessary and find the optimal distance between poles for your horse. You can also adjust the distance by riding small, medium, and large circles over the fan. Go a little toward the outer edge of the poles, and the distances are greater, while closer to the "point" and the distance is quite short.

When leading your horse over the fan, walk beside him at first, then "longe" him around you as you stand at the "point." Give him enough rope so that he can travel over the last third of the poles, toward the "open" end, first. Let him do this larger circle and greater distance between poles turn two or three times before you ask him for the smaller circle and attempt the middle of the poles, where the distances between poles are shorter.

HOW TO DO IT

Make sure you are straight coming into the first pole, and give the reins a little forward so that your horse can better assess the fan layout before him. When in the fan, the horse must bend according to the size of the turn you are riding. Make sure you turn your body to help "show him" the way!

Typical mistakes in this exercise include the rider collapsing at the hip, resulting in the horse "falling out" over his shoulder. It is also common for the horse to "push" toward the "point" of the fan.

You can address these issues by not overturning your inside shoulder and hip (closer to the "point") in the turn, but rather keeping your weight a little to the outside. Pay attention to your inside leg. It shouldn't be too passive and must clearly support the horse. And, don't inadvertently pull the horse toward the "point" with the inside rein.

Tip

You have the opportunity to improve your horse's flexibility and rhythm in the fan. To do so, it is best to begin with three poles and increase up to a maximum of five poles, as mentioned on p. 42.

This is not an easy exercise for the horse because he must go over the poles while traveling on a smoothly bent line. He must not only organize his body for the turn, he needs to pay attention to his legs and feet so he doesn't stumble. When both of you are ready, you can make the exercise even more difficult by raising the poles on one end.

1 Romeo is a small horse and so quite easily masters a smaller circle close to the "point" of the fan, stepping carefully between each pole with even bend in his body.

2 When you reach the end of the fan, ride straight over the last pole and continue your circle.

3 When "longeing" your horse over the poles at the trot, give him plenty of rope so he can reach the middle or far end of the poles where the distances are greatest.

Crossed Poles Square ●●●

It takes four ground poles to build this exercise. Lay each pole so that one end is on the ground and the other end lies on top of another pole. The poles should be about 6½ feet (2 meters) apart—vary this distance as needed according to the size of your horse. Obviously, the poles will need to be farther apart for a large warmblood than for a pony.

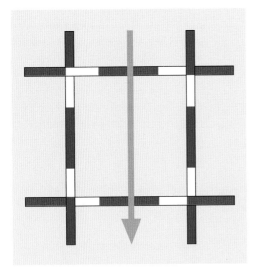

Even though Romeo has mastered this exercise, he still looks where he steps.

WHAT IT LOOKS LIKE

You have a lot of possibilities with the crossed poles square. You can simply ride over the poles; you can ride in, halt, and turn in the center before exiting; you can ride circles or voltes that cross the obstacle at its corners; or you can ride diagonally across the square.

First, lead or ride your horse at the walk on a long rein through the crossed poles square. Make sure that you go exactly across the middle of the poles. Let your horse stretch forward and downward, and walk briskly but relaxed through the figure.

As soon as your horse can go straight over the poles without a problem, make it more difficult by trotting over the poles. The horse should still move fluidly—he should not slow or rush over the poles.

Romeo remains straight inside the crossed poles square exercises. I should "give" more with my hands here so his nose could be more forward.

HOW TO DO IT

When leading the horse from the ground, make sure he stays with you and walks straight and briskly over the poles without swinging his front or back end to the right or left. If your horse starts to get crooked over the poles, stop immediately and begin again. Try to correct your horse's position outside the crossed poles obstacle, if possible, to avoid confusing him.

When riding, sit in a supple and relaxed way in the saddle, and "give" your reins a hands' breadth forward so your horse can stretch. Make sure that he steps evenly and without hesitation over both poles.

I give Romeo a lot of rein. He can and should stretch forward in this exercise.

Crossed Poles Square: Diagonal ●●●

In this variation of the exercise you learned on p. 44, you don't ride across the middle of the poles in and out of the square, but rather from one corner to the other. This is difficult because the horse must lengthen his stride where the two poles are crossed over one another in each corner. The first few times the horse might bump a pole. Ignore it at first. With more practice the horse will improve. Note that depending on the size of your horse, you might need to make the crossed poles square larger.

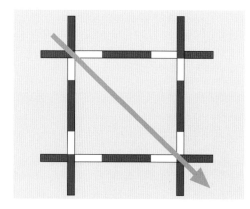

Romeo and I step over one crossed corner of the obstacle, entering the interior of the square on the diagonal.

WHAT IT LOOKS LIKE

Enter this exercise coming straight into the open "V" formed by the crossed ends of two of the poles in the square, then cross the inside of the obstacle on the diagonal, exiting straight through the crossed ends of the poles directly opposite your entry point.

Before you approach the obstacle, let the horse take a good look at it. The goal is for him to cross the poles willingly, without hesitation or hurry, so don't rush the introduction.

HOW TO DO IT

When practicing the exercise from the ground, approach one corner of the obstacle at your horse's side. Let the lead rope hang loose and don't hurry your horse. If your horse steps incorrectly over the crossed poles or tries to swing either his front end or hindquarters out, stop and start over again. Your goal is for him to remain straight on the diagonal. If your horse continues to go over the crossed poles crookedly, ask a friend to walk with you and correct the horse's position from the opposite side.

When riding, make sure you prepare the horse for a straight entry over the crossed poles in the corner of the square. If it seems like he wants to avoid the corner, correct his position with your weight and leg aids promptly. Only use your reins as a last resort. If your horse doesn't step correctly over the crossed poles the first time, it's not a big deal. Try the exercise again and ride with a bit more focus toward the poles. You must keep your concentration, too!

If your horse is hesitant about going over the crossed poles at the corners and consis-

tently veers right or left in your approach, try breaking down the exercise: Ride up to the corner, stand straight and quiet in front of it, and praise your horse. Then ask him to take a step more so that only his front legs are over the crossed poles. Again ask him to halt and stand straight and quiet. Praise him. Then ride all the way into the square and cross the diagonaly, but before stepping out at the next corner, repeat the "stand straight and quiet" steps. By the second or third time through, you won't need to stop any more—your horse will be able to do it in one fluid motion.

You can see that Romeo and I are both concentrating and keeping our eyes on the goal of entering the obstacle over the crossed ends of the poles. He is nice and straight.

Romeo steps confidently out over the corner of the crossed poles square. I support him with my leg aids and give him a long rein so he steps straight and remains nice and forward over the crossed poles.

Crossed Poles Square: Volte ••●

To improve your horse's longitudinal bend from nose to tail, you can train with voltes (or larger circles) over the crossed poles square. Depending on the size of the volte or circle, the poles will be closer to or farther from one another. Ride voltes in both directions, but always start in the direction that is easier for your horse. Just like people, horses have one side on which they bend more easily, and so tend to prefer traveling in one direction over the other. You can improve the horse's stiff side using this exercise, and the result will be that your horse becomes straighter in all that you do.

WHAT IT LOOKS LIKE

Before you begin, consider the size of volte that would be best for your horse—6, 8, or 10 meters in diameter—and arrange the crossed poles square appropriately for that distance. The simplest variation, and a good way to start, is to ride your horse in a large circle that includes going over the whole crossed poles square to let your horse adjust to the exercise. Then move on to the smaller voltes.

HOW TO DO IT

From the ground, lead your horse in a small circle that uses one crossed corner as its center, or stand at the crossed corner and ask your horse to circle around you, as if longeing him. Make sure your horse bends evenly through his body.

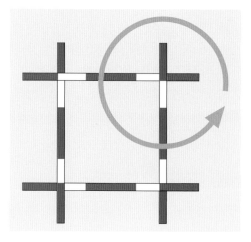

I maintain Romeo's bend with light aids.

When riding, the diameter of the volte determines greater or lesser longitudinal bend in your horse. The smaller the volte being ridden, the more balanced and collected the horse must be. His forefeet and hind feet should travel the same path.

Even on a smaller volte, do not take the inside rein (inside the bend) too short and never pull on it. This is not only painful to the horse but also blocks his inside hind leg so it can't step further under the horse's body, which unbalances the horse.

Be sure you don't ask too much and end up in a fight with your horse. If the exercise doesn't work at first, take a few steps back and start over. Go back to the big circle to start, then try as large a volte as possible. Bend and balance require concentration from your horse, so while it may seem like an easy exercise, it is important to recognize how much work it is for him. Reward him now and then with a break, and ride him on a relaxed long rein around the arena.

You can clearly see the bend in Romeo's whole body as we cross the poles in a volte.

Common mistakes in this exercise include the rider not preparing the horse sufficiently; the rider exaggerating the position of the horse, overflexing or overbending him; the rider holding too tightly with her inside hand, sacrificing the horse's rhythm and impulsion; and the horse swinging his hindquarters out in the turn.

Most problems can be solved by always warming your horse up, first with generous circles and then large voltes, before trying something more challenging. It is necessary to pay attention to your seat and consciously maintain a soft, playful contact with the inside rein, nothing more. You can prevent the hind end from falling out by keeping your outside leg back a little behind the girth in a "guarding" position.

Romeo carefully lifts his feet over the poles in the obstacle.

Crossed Poles Square: Figure Eight ●●○

Another great way to use the crossed poles square is to ride a figure eight over the opposing corners of the obstacle, changing rein in the middle of the square's interior. This exercise requires the horse to respond lightly to the rider's aids because there is very little room for a soft change of direction, which should occur exactly in the middle of the square. In this small space the horse's hindquarters must step well under his center of gravity.

HOW TO DO IT

When leading the horse through the exercise from the ground, watch carefully how he moves. He should bend evenly and in a supple way in both directions.

Use large voltes (see p. 30) as the "top" and "bottom" of your figure eight at first, and practice the transition from one direction to the other a couple of times. Try to achieve a soft, fluid change of direction, even from the ground.

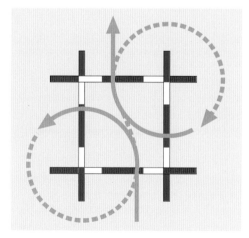

My outside leg is in a "guarding" position, a little back behind the girth. This is keeps the horse's hind end on the bending line of the figure eight.

When riding, have the horse collected enough to allow you to straighten him in the middle of the square for one or two steps before asking him to bend in the new direction. Your aids for the bending lines must be light and fluid. Don't pull your horse around the corner with your inside rein. Ride round, flowing curves. Lay your inside leg (inside the bend) softly against the horse to encourage him to bend around it.

As with other exercises, if the figure eight doesn't work at first, leave the crossed poles square altogether, ride around the arena for a moment, and start over. Don't fight with your horse in the obstacle. That will only confuse him and possibly ruin the exercise for you in the future.

Try this exercise at the trot when you and your horse can do it easily at the walk. But don't circle in and out of the crossed poles square endlessly! An occasional trip around the arena at the trot with a nice stretch on a long rein relaxes and rewards both horse and rider.

1 When aiding for one of the voltes in the figure eight, your inside leg lies softly at the girth (note that my knee could be lower if I did a better job stretching my inside leg long here).
2 Your weight should be slightly to the inside.
3 Your hips and shoulders should turn with the horse along the path of the volte.

Cavalletti on the Circle ●●●

You can longe or ride the horse on a circle **over cavalletti (raised poles on short standards at varying low heights). This teaches your horse that he can't simply run around a circle, or lazily amble, but must pay attention to his legs and where he is stepping. For this exercise place two cavalletti on your circle—one on each side, opposite each other, so the horse walks or trots a half-circle before reaching an obstacle.**

As I longe Shir Khan on a circle over cavalletti, my leading hand (right) indicates the direction and the other hand drives him forward (here, my left). It is beautiful to see how Shir Khan bends around me.

WHAT IT LOOKS LIKE

As described, start with two cavalletti on the circle, placed across from each other. The appropriate height for cavalletti at the walk or trot is 6 to 8 inches (15 to 20 centimeters). Longe the horse at a walk over the poles, in both directions. Then try it at the trot. Do the same thing when in the saddle. If you like, you can also do this exercise at the canter. The height of cavalletti should be increased to 20 inches (50 centimeters) when circling at the canter.

HOW TO DO IT

When longeing over the cavalletti, make sure you send the horse to the middle of each pole so he doesn't try to evade the obstacle, stopping or running past it to one side. It can help to add a clear voice or hand signal to indicate the change of rhythm and/or tempo when he reaches the cavalletti.

If your horse does evade to the inside, send him back out on the circle with your leading hand. Most horses try to run outside the cavalletti, which you can prevent with proper management of the length of your lead rope or longe line.

Help send your horse over the cavalletti with a clear voice command. Here Shir Khan jumps it, which is okay.

After a successful session in hand, I let Shir Khan relax with a walk around the arena.

As when longeing, you need to make sure your horse goes straight to the middle of the cavalletti when riding him. Keep your horse on the circle and straight over the cavalletti with your weight and leg aids. Your weight should be slightly to the inside (inside the bend) and your inside leg at the girth. Be sure you don't collapse your hip because that shoves your weight to the outside! Your outside leg is positioned a little back behind the girth in a "guarding" position to help maintain the longitudinal bend. Encourage your horse to bend through his neck and shoulder region by lightly vibrating the inside rein.

Cavalletti and Ground Poles ●●○

Cavalletti bring a lot of flexibility to training because they are so adjust-
able. Their varying height (see p. 52) causes the horse to lift his legs
more actively than he does when going over ground poles alone. You can
bring further variety to your training by combining cavalletti and ground
poles in one exercise.

WHAT IT LOOKS LIKE

These exercises are
especially demanding
for the horse. Arrange a
line alternating ground
poles and cavalletti. The
distance between the
poles and the height of the
cavalletti must be appro-
priate for the gait and the
individual horse (see pp.
22 and 52).

When moving through
a line of ground poles
alternating with caval-
letti, your horse must pay
close attention to his legs
and feet. Begin with a
basic combination of three
elements: ground pole,
cavalletto, ground pole.
Later, as you and your
horse grow more confi-
dent, increase the number
of poles and cavalletti.

Work over poles and cavalletti
develops impulsion and hind leg
activity. Many horses also become
more supple with this kind of
exercise.

HOW TO DO IT

When beginning on the ground, leading your horse, give him enough rope so he can stretch forward with his head and neck. Walk briskly over the poles and cavalletto. When all is well, try walking alongside him at a distance, as he goes over the poles and cavalletto on his own. When your horse has mastered the exercise at the walk, practice it at the trot.

As with other pole exercises, it is important to help your horse travel straight down the middle so it is less likely he will try to evade the exercise. If you notice him hesitating or veering sideways, correct it quickly with your leading hand and driving hand, then let the lead rope hang loose again as he moves forward.

If the exercise falls completely apart, just start over from the beginning.

When riding, start at the walk and let your horse find his own tempo over the poles and cavalletto. At first your horse might knock the cavalletto, but as soon as he understands the difference between the cavalletto and the ground poles, he will learn to adjust his stride so he can walk over them without hitting them. Don't get impatient; let your horse take his time and find his way.

As you travel down the middle of the poles, "give" the reins forward. If your horse tries to evade to one side or the other, promptly correct him with your leg and weight aids.

1 "Give" your hands a little forward as you trot over the ground poles and cavalletto so your horse has room to adjust his head and neck and see what is lying before him.
2 Ride straight and forward as you exit the obstacle. The horse should move willingly and smoothly over the poles.

Training Exercises with Cones

Cones provide endless exercise possibilities, from the very simple to the difficult. A few ideas are presented on the following pages. Almost all the exercises I recommend gymnasticize the horse. In addition, the horse learns to pay attention to your signals and react with sensitivity to your aids. The rider learns "feel" and to give the aids with more precision. The exercises with cones that I provide require dexterity. Weight and leg aids are very important. These are also great exercises to strengthen concentration and coordination in both horse and rider.

If possible, have between four and twelve traffic cones on hand. This will allow you almost limitless possibilities in terms of setup. The cones should be made of flexible material. They must be stable and they should not tear if the horse rides over them. If you don't have cones, you can use buckets, instead.

There are many possible variations to the exercises ahead. You can go forward or backward around the cones. You can ride voltes, figure eights, and half-passes between the cones. The turn-on-the-forehand and turn-on-the-haunches can be practiced with cones, as well as spiraling circles (gradually enlarging your bending line and then reducing it).

Don't feel limited to the exercises I describe here. Cones are very useful in many training and riding scenarios. You can use cones to mark your riding path and provide visual focal points. You can use cones to create a well-marked road to help keep you straight. You can place cones in each corner of your arena to remind you to ride deep in your corners. Or you can use them to help you make precise transitions. Go ahead and be creative!

Volte around a Cone ●●●

You will find your voltes are easy to make perfectly round when
you ride them around a cone! Watch how quickly you improve
your voltes with this simple exercise. On your first try, notice
how much your distance from the cone in the center of your
volte varies. Often the horse reduces the size of the volte in
the second half without the rider noticing. A cone in the center
helps you and your horse learn to travel in a symmetrical circle
with an even bend all the way around.

WHAT IT LOOKS LIKE

As you learned on p. 30, a volte is a circle with
a diameter of 6, 8, or 10 meters. The horse
bends longitudinally from nose to tail along
this line. His hind hooves should travel in the
tracks of his front hooves.

When you practice voltes around a cone,
remember that the smaller the circle, the
more difficult the exercise is for the horse.
Always start with larger voltes and increase
the difficulty (by decreasing the size) gradually. Try to use primarily weight and leg aids;
do not rely on your reins. Ride two to four
voltes around a cone at the walk, then take a
break and ride around the whole arena so the
horse can stretch and relax before you begin
again.

When you can travel perfectly round, even
voltes of different sizes using only your weight
and leg aids at the walk, try the exercise at
the trot.

Voltes at the canter require the horse to be
well balanced and able to bring his hindquarters well under him. For most riders, it is
better to concentrate on riding voltes well at
the walk and trot, and this translates to other
parts of their riding.

Use the cone as a reference point when you ride a volte
around it. This will help you get a better feeling for distance and how to ride round voltes with a consistent bend
in the horse.

HOW TO DO IT

When riding a volte to the left, for example, around a cone, take your outside (right) leg a little back behind the girth to prevent the horse's hindquarters from swinging out. Your inside (left) leg drives the horse forward at the girth. Turn your upper body in the direction of the movement on the bending line your horse is traveling, but keep your eyes on the cone in the middle. Your weight should be a bit to the inside, but don't collapse at the hip. Keep yourself straight! Your inside rein should maintain the horse's flexion, while your outside rein supports him and prevents his shoulder from falling out.

After you've practiced this exercise a bit and feel confident, try riding the volte with the reins in one hand. Keep your body straight and your horse on an even, bending line with only your leg and weight aids.

Silke looks at the cone in the center of her volte. Her whole body follows the bending line on which her horse is traveling. When the rider's weight and leg aids are correct, the horse bends almost automatically.

Volte with a Stick ●●●

Dexterity is required in this exercise. **You need a traffic cone that is open at the top, and a stick of some kind with a length of thin rope about 6½ feet (2 meters) long tied to one end. A stiff dressage whip or horseman's stick (there are many kind's available on the market) works perfectly.**

It requires a lot of coordination to ride a well-formed volte one-handed.

There are different ways to hold the reins in one hand, depending on your discipline and preference. In this exercise, use the method you are most comfortable with.

WHAT THE EXERCISE LOOKS LIKE

Place the cone so it is in an appropriate position to be the middle of your volte. Next position the stick or whip, complete with the length of rope, into the top opening of the cone. The rope should hang free.

Ride up to the cone and grasp the free end of the rope. Ride out as far as the rope allows you. Holding the end of the rope in your inside (inside the volte) hand, try to ride an even, round volte around the cone. The rope should be stretched taut but the stick should not come out of the cone and the cone should not fall over.

The difficulty lies in relying on your weight and leg aids while trying to organize the volte at the end of the rope. Try the exercise in both directions. It looks easier than it is, as you will see!

HOW TO DO IT

Your weight and leg aids are of the utmost importance in this exercise. Use the reins as little as possible. Hold your horse on a small volte with weight aids (shifted to the inside of the volte) and leg aids (outside leg slightly behind the girth, inside leg at the girth). Correct only minimally with the hands. Use your body in the turn as you look toward the cone and concentrate on keeping the stick in it and the cone upright.

Those who ride Western may find this exercise a bit easier, since they and their horses may be accustomed to neck-reining (the horse reacts to the touch of the outside rein on his neck). If you are unfamiliar with riding one-handed, hold the reins in whichever hand is on the outside of the volte (the inside hand holds the rope) between your thumb and the index finger or between your index and middle finger. The hand should remain quiet; it should not cross over the horse's mane. Even if your horse does not neck-rein,

it is possible to send signals through the reins through sensitive flexion and giving of the fingers. For example, a yield of one rein is possible by stretching or loosening the fingers that on that rein.

When you have a good feel for the exercise and your horse is bending well, try it at the trot. Your horse will try to make the volte around the cone larger. The faster the pace, the more difficult it is for him to maintain the bend on the tighter turn. To prevent your horse from evading to the outside so he can travel on a larger (easier, for him) arc, bring your outside leg back to keep his hind end in line and control the outside shoulder with the outside rein. Remember: Never pull on the inside rein to make a volte smaller as it blocks the horse's inside hind leg from stepping well up and under him, and the exercise becomes useless.

Some find this exercise more successful when they sit the trot. It depends on you and your horse, however, so try it both sitting and posting.

Exercise 30: Stick in the Cone Variation

Another and more difficult variation of this exercise is to hold the stick in your hand and try to get it, or the end of the rope, in the opening at the top of the cone as you walk by. At the beginning you can halt your horse beside the cone, but challenge yourself to get it at the walk. This is difficult enough on a straight line, but you can also ride a volte around the cone as just described in Exercise 29.

Sometimes what seems like just a playful game can actually be very difficult. With a little creativity, you will see that training can be fun for both you and your horse!

Figure Eight with Two Cones ●●○

Place two cones about 10 to 13 feet (3 to 4 meters) apart. You will ride simple figure eights around them. The ideal space between the cones really depends on the size and level of training of your horse: The cones might need to be farther apart, or maybe closer together.

This exercise is a reasonable next step if you have successfully ridden the simple voltes around the cones in Exercises 28 and 29 (see pp. 58 and 60).

Canter voltes are for advanced riders and require a very well-balanced horse.

WHAT IT LOOKS LIKE

It's best to start with the cones far enough apart that you can work easily at both the walk and the trot. When you and your horse are ready to do the figure eight at the canter, increase the distance between the cones and you should feel comfortable doing a simple or flying change.

Ride a large volte around the first cone. When you reach the point where you began, at the midpoint between the two cones, straighten your horse, let him take two or three steps, and then introduce the new bend for the next volte around the second cone. This creates a figure eight with two symmetrical halves. Concentrate on making the individual circles really round. Ride both circles with discipline, using the tips you learned in Exercise 28 (see p. 58).

Riding figure eights improves longitudinal bend in your horse. In addition, he is evenly gymnasticized and his suppleness is improved. As with other exercises, every now and then you should ride around the whole arena on a long rein so that your horse stretches and relaxes.

HOW TO DO IT

Start at the walk, and practice getting the bend in each direction using primarily your weight and leg aids. How much rein contact do you need? If your horse loses the bend, you must naturally take up the reins. The flexion left or right must always be maintained or the exercise is worthless as a means of gymnasticizing and suppling the horse's body.

Turn your upper body in the direction of the movement—so if your first volte is to the right, turn it slightly right. Take a little more on the inside (right) rein with your inside leg at the girth and your outside (left) leg a little back behind the girth. At the point of the change of direction, straighten the horse for two strides or so, then reverse your aids to send him in the new direction. Give the aids softly.

When you are ready to try this exercise at the trot, it is easier to sit it. If the training level of your horse allows, you can then try the exercise at the canter, beginning with a simple change and moving on to a flying change if you are an advanced enough rider.

As you come around the volte, be sure that your horse's head doesn't go too deep, as shown here.

Exercise 32: Voltes with Two Cones Variation

Instead of doing a figure eight, an easier variation of this exercise is to begin by riding a volte around the first cone, then ride straight down the "long side" to where the volte around the next cone should begin. Upon completing the second volte, again ride down the "long side" back to the first cone.

In this case you don't have to change the flexion and bend, and you can keep the horse straight longer between voltes, making this exercise simpler for you both.

Try it at all three gaits.

Serpentine with Three Cones ●●●

Now and then it is nice to work this simple exercise with three cones into your training. Place the cones as shown below and ride serpentines between them. This supples the horse at the walk and the trot. You can also ride serpentines at the canter if you have enough room between cones and have mastered the simple or flying change.

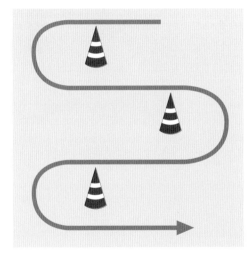

The amount of flexion and bend in the horse should correspond to the size of the serpentine loop.

WHAT IT LOOKS LIKE

Place two cones in a straight line about 26 to 33 feet (8 to 10 meters) apart. Stride half the distance between the two cones, turn to the right or left, and stride 13 feet (4 meters) off the line. Place your third cone here. Make sure you have enough distance between the cone and the arena wall or fence for you to ride around it in the serpentine pattern. Ride serpentines at the walk and trot around the three cones.

HOW TO DO IT

When riding serpentines, you have to change the horse's flexion and bend after every cone. Shift your seat slightly in the direction of the movement. Your inside leg and inside rein (inside the bend) create the flexion and bend. The outside rein and leg (outside the bend) prevent the horse's shoulder and hindquarters from falling out.

Cloverleaf with Three Cones ●●●

As you are now aware, **repeated, smooth changes of bend in each direction are very useful for gymnasticizing the horse.** Longitudinal bend to the left and right requires contraction and relaxation of the horse's muscles, and the alternation between both strengthens and supples the body. Riding bending lines correctly also helps the horse become straighter in all that you do.

WHAT IT LOOKS LIKE

With the cones set up as they were for ser- pentines (see p. 64), begin in the middle of the three cones and ride a volte to the left around the "top" cone. Proceed like you are riding a figure eight, changing bend in the middle and beginning a volte to the right around the "bot- tom" cone. When you are again in the middle, ride the horse straight a couple of strides and then into a volte to the left around the "middle" cone. End the exercise where you started, in the middle of the three cones.

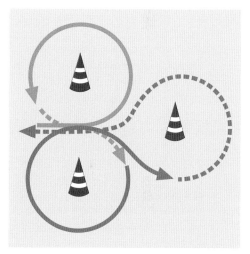

HOW TO DO IT

The aids for this exercise are the same as with the previous exercises that include voltes and changes of direction. You must use the outside (outside the bend) aids to support the horse on the volte while the inside rein and leg create the bend. Sit a little more on the inside seat bone. Look at the cone you are circling!

Apply the aids quietly and with the right timing so you prepare the horse for the movement and so he knows what direction he is going next. Adjust your seat promptly. Weight, leg, and reins aids must be given just before the point at which you want to change direction.

Turn-on-the-Forehand and Turn-on-the-Haunches with Cones ●●●

This is a demanding exercise. **You need three cones and will be practicing changes of direction. Your horse might be a little surprised at first by the exercise, but he will quickly learn to concentrate on your signals and wait for your next cue.**

WHAT IT LOOKS LIKE

Place three cones in your riding area so they form a large triangle.

Ride to the first cone, halt when the horse's front end is a little ways past the cone, and make a turn-on-the-forehand of about 90 degrees (the horse's hind end makes a quarter-circle around his front legs, which remain almost in place). Halt again when you are facing in the direction of the next cone in the triangle. Wait for a moment, then ride to the second cone and a little ways past it with the horse's front end. Make another turn-on-the-forehand of about 90 degrees until you are facing the third cone in the triangle. Ride to the last cone and repeat the exercise.

The same exercise can be ridden using the turn-on-the-haunches at each cone. To do this, ride to the first cone and halt when the horse's hindquarters are just beyond the cone. Do a turn-on-the-haunches of about 90 degrees (the horse's forehand moves in a quarter-circle around the hindquarters, which remain almost in place), until you are facing the next cone. Pause briefly, then ride to the next cone in the triangle, and repeat the exercise. If you like, you can also mix it up, riding the turn-on-the-forehand and the turn-on-the-haunches interchangeably.

Here you can see how wide the horse's hind legs are stepping as the turn-on-the-forehand is performed at the cone.

HOW TO DO IT

You need to apply the weight and leg aids accurately for this exercise to be effective. With the turn-on-the-forehand, flex the horse with the inside rein (away from the direction of movement—so if you're traveling toward the right as in the photos, your left rein) so that you can see his eye. Weight your inside (left) seat bone. Your inside leg drives from a little behind the girth while the outside (right) leg maintains a "guarding" position to prevent the hindquarters from moving around the forehand too quickly or imprecisely. The outside rein limits the horse's movement of the front end and prevents his shoulder from popping out. Look in the direction you are moving the haunches. Maintain contact. If your horse moves forward, take up the reins a little. If your horse moves backward, apply your outside leg a little. If he steps around too quickly, take a half-halt on the outside rein.

When riding a turn-on-the-haunches, the rein on the side of the direction you are traveling must "show the horse the way." If you are asking the horse to do a turn-on-the-haunches to the right, for example, weight your inside (right) seat bone. The inside rein introduces the turn, and your inside leg drives the horse forward at the girth. Your outside (left) leg causes the horse's front legs to step around the turn. The outside rein limits the bend, but not so much that you block the horse's ability to step around the turn.

Praise your horse after every successful turn, and don't practice this exercise for too long without a break to stretch and relax.

With the turn-on-the-forehand at the cone, the horse's hind end moves around the forehand. The rider sits straight and tall. Note the distance between the cones is fairly short here—you can set up your cone triangle at any size that suits your horse and the lesson.

The horse should move his hindquarters in a quarter-circle without shifting forward or backward.

Spiraling In and Out with Cones ●●●

You need between eight and twelve cones for this exercise. Place them in your riding area as depicted in the diagram below. For the inside and smallest circle, the cones should be placed at least 16 to 20 feet (5 to 6 meters) from one another. Even if you want to ride a very small circle in the center, it is better to make the distance a little bit larger than to make it too tight. Delineate the next circle with cones at least 10 feet (3 meters) out from the first ones (or about four giant steps).

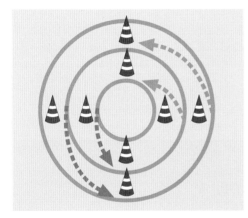

Beginning with the largest circle, ride at the walk around the outside of the cones.

WHAT IT LOOKS LIKE

If you use eight cones you will have a very small circle inside the first set of cones, a small to medium circle outside the first set of cones, and then a large circle outside the second set of cones. Twelve cones enable you to have a still larger circle beyond that if you have enough room in your arena to work with.

Ride around the outside of the cones marking the largest circle. When the first circle is completed, use your seat, legs, and reins to guide the horse in onto the next size (slightly smaller) circle, and ride between the cones delineating the outermost circle and the cones marking the innermost circle. Continue all the way in to the smallest circle in the middle. After the second time around the innermost circle, leg-yield out to enlarge the circle again, going around each "layer" of cones until you again reach the largest circle on the outside. Don't rush. Give your horse time to get used to this exercise and find the appropriate bend at each circle size.

After you have gone through the exercise several times at the walk in both directions, try it at the trot. You will find that at increased speed it is not easy to stay within the limits of the cones. This exercise is very difficult at the canter since the change from a large circle to a smaller one comes very fast. For most horses, the inside circle shouldn't be too small at the canter, as the smaller the circle, the more collection and "loading" of the hindquarters is required.

HOW TO DO IT

Using the techniques you learned to ride a round volte (see p. 30), ask for the correct flexion and bend and ride a forward walk around the largest circle. As you gradually reduce the size of the circle, the horse will need a certain level of "positive body tension" in order to increase his longitudinal bend on the decreasing circle size. Support him with your inside (inside the bend) leg at the girth, your inside rein asking for flexion, and your outside leg and rein keeping the hindquarters and outside shoulder in line. Sit more to the inside and use a bit more outside leg as you decrease the size of the circle. When you are ready, use the aids for the leg-yield (see p. 12) to increase the size of the circle, moving progressively out from the smallest to the largest.

Once you have practiced this at the walk and trot, you can ride the exercise at the canter to further improve your horse's suppleness and balance. At the canter, make sure that the bend of the horse conforms to the size of the circle—it is harder at this gait. The bend on the smallest circle will be significant, but you don't want only the horse's neck to bend around while the rest of him falls out over his shoulder. His inside hind leg must step well under his center of gravity.

1 Progressively reducing the circle size at the canter promotes an active inside hind leg in the horse.
2 Silke and Danubio canter one-handed on a beautiful bending line.

The Four-Leaf Clover ●●●

The four-leaf clover is a great way **to gymnasticize your horse and keep things interesting, using voltes in a simple pattern.**

Place four cones in square shape in the arena. The cones will serve as center-points, around which voltes will be ridden. This variation makes daily schooling more fun and increases the horse's attention to the sensitive aids of the rider.

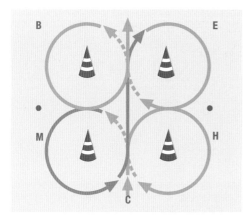

around the first cone to your left. Return to the centerline and ride a few strides straight ahead until you are across from the second cone to your right. Repeat the pattern you just rode, completing a volte to the right, returning to the centerline to change the bend, and riding a volte around the final cone to your left.

Finish the four-leaf clover by walking or trotting straight ahead on the centerline at X in a straight line.

HOW TO DO IT

Begin at the walk, move on to the trot when the walk seems easy, and try the exercise at the canter when you are very confident in your horse's focus and your own riding ability.

It is important in this exercise to prepare your horse at the right time for a change of bend. Think about your weight and leg aids; stay erect in the saddle. Try to ensure that the horse doesn't fall out over his shoulder or swing his haunches to the outside.

As is the case with many exercises in this book, the four-leaf clover looks easier than it is. It takes a lot of concentration on the part of horse and rider to complete this exercise well. And as you increase speed or gait, you must be more precise about the timing of your aids.

WHAT IT LOOKS LIKE

In one half of your riding area or arena, place your four cones in a square shape, with equal distances between each. My recommended distance between the cones is between 20 and 30 feet (6 to 9 meters) or 8 to 12 giant steps.

Begin the exercise by riding from what would be the letter "C" on the short side of a dressage arena up the centerline (see diagram). Focus on your first cone to the right, and ride a volte around it (see p. 30 for instructions on riding voltes around a single cone). As soon as you are back on the centerline, change the bend and make a left volte

Four-Leaf Clover: Shoulder-In ●●○

Instead of riding simple voltes **around the four cones, you can add a few steps of shoulder-in. This exercise has a wonderful suppling effect on the horse.**

WHAT IT LOOKS LIKE

The shoulder-in is a fundamental lateral movement and important for every horse and rider. Riding it as part of a volte in the same four-leaf clover pattern you used in Exercise 37 (p. 70) provides variety in training, as well as keeping the cones as useful reference points and pathmakers.

In shoulder-in, the horse's hindquarters stay on one track or path, and his forehand is brought inside that track as he displays a slight bend away from the direction in which he is moving (forward). The horse's inside foreleg (inside the bend) passes and crosses in front of his outside foreleg, and his inside hind leg steps in the same path as the outside foreleg.

HOW TO DO IT

Add a few steps of shoulder-in to each volte before continuing the four-leaf clover pattern and moving on to the next cone. The volte helps you establish the correct bend for the shoulder-in. Halfway around the volte, "hold" the position from the volte but take a few steps forward rather than continuing on the circle—the horse's hindquarters are on one track and his shoulders are "inside" in a shoulder-in. Your inside leg (inside the bend) is at the girth, your outside leg is in the "guarding" position behind the girth to keep the hindquarters from swinging out, your inside seat bone is weighted, and your inside positioning rein keeps and controls the bend you acquired on the volte while working with the outside rein to indicate direction and placement of the horse's shoulders.

Watch that your horse doesn't just bend his neck around as you ask for the steps of shoulder-in. His inside hind leg (inside the bend) must also step actively forward. After a few steps forward, finish the volte, change direction on the centerline, and go on to the next cone.

The shoulder-in is a key exercise for the correct gymnasticization of the horse. It requires sensitive coordination of your weight, leg, and rein aids.

Half-Pass between Cones ●●●

Has it ever occurred to you to practice a lateral movement like the half-pass with the help of cones? Well, you can! The cones serve as reference points to help the rider focus on where she is going as she is busy thinking about the aids for the movement. You will need six cones arranged in groups of two on a diagonal line with a distance between each pair of 16½ to 26 feet (5 to 8 meters). At the walk, ride the half-pass between the cones. Eventually, you can try the exercise at the trot.

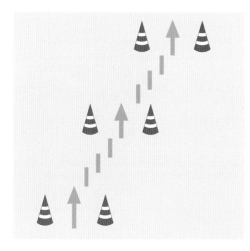

WHAT IT LOOKS LIKE

Ride straight through the first pair of cones at a walk. After a horse's body length, begin the half-pass, moving forward and sideways, until you reach the next set of cones. Just before the cones, straighten your horse and ride straight through them. About a horse's body length on the other side, begin the half-pass again to the third set of cones. Try it in both direction. Then walk the horse around the arena on a long rein.

You can see Silke's aids as she finishes the half-pass to the right and prepares to straighten her horse before going through the cones.

In the half-pass, the horse bends in the direction of travel, and his forehand slightly leads his hind end.

Both the horse's front and hind legs cross in the half-pass.

In the half-pass, the horse is bent in the direction of travel, and his forehand moves slightly in advance of his hindquarters. His outside legs (outside the bend) pass and cross in front of his inside legs as he moves forward and sideways on a diagonal path.

HOW TO DO IT

When riding the half-pass, the rider shifts her weight in the direction of the movement. For example, if the horse is moving to the right in the half-pass, as in the diagram and photos, the rider sits to the right. In addition, the horse is flexed and bent to the right (the inside) with the rider's right (inside) rein. Your inside leg is at the girth to maintain the bend and forward movement, and your outside (left) leg, is held behind the girth to control the position and angle of the horse's hind end. The outside rein works with the inside leg to indicate speed and path of travel.

Ending on a Good Note

It's good to take time to allow yourself and your horse to relax after you have worked on an exercise or exercises that required intense concentration. End an exercise when you have done it well once or twice, or if your horse has tried hard to do as you've asked (even if it wasn't 100 percent perfect) and take walk on a long rein. Don't forget to praise your horse, and time your praise so it connects with a job well done, because that motivates the horse and shows him that he is on the right track.

A GOOD TIME TO *STOP*

When training the horse, it is important that you do not miss a good time to stop. As you may already know: When you end an exercise on a good note it is easier to come back and build on it later. When an exercise hasn't gone well and you end frustrated or annoyed with your horse, and he too is frustrated or annoyed, neither of you will want to work at it again in the future.

By telling your horse, "Good boy!" and letting him rest at the right time, you help him stay motivated. In actual practice that can mean that you end a training session after only a single, short exercise. If it was a really good exercise, ending there

is far better than repeating the exercise so much that all energy and concentration are soon depleted and both horse and rider only want to get away—from the exercise and each other.

I'd like to show you a few ways I like to end training sessions on a positive note.

Naturally, as mentioned throughout this book, you can simply ride at the walk on a long rein a few times around the arena or go for a little trail ride as a relaxing reward. But if you are looking for other ideas, see which of the following appeal to you.

Playing Ball ●●●

To end a training session on a softer, friendlier note, choose an exercise that is fun and less stressful for you and your horse. You can find large horse-safe balls (available through many tack and equipment retailers) to add a bit of "play" to the day. Introduce your horse to the ball first from the ground so he gets used to it and isn't frightened by the ball when you approach it with you in the saddle.

WHAT IT LOOKS LIKE

In hand, show your horse the ball and how it moves so he gets used to the rolling object. If he is relaxed and curious, set out two cones or two empty buckets to mark a "goal" in the riding arena, and encourage your horse to nudge or "kick" the ball with his front legs through the goal. It doesn't matter if the horse moves the ball with his legs or his nose. Try the same thing from the saddle.

HOW TO DO IT

From the ground, lead your horse directly up to the ball. Do not stand in front of the ball. If something frightens your horse, he might try to jump over it. Allow him to sniff and explore the ball to get over any fear.

Praise your horse when he pushes the ball with his nose or leg.

Many horses spook when the ball hits them on the back of the legs or rolls against their belly. That can be dangerous when you are riding, so once the horse is comfortable with approaching the ball and standing near it, roll the ball slowly toward him, introducing him to the feel of the ball against his body. Repeat until the horse shows no sign of spooking at the sight, sound, or feel of the ball.

From the saddle, try to direct your horse toward the ball using only your weight and leg aids. Leave the reins loose as much as possible. After a while, you will find the horse concentrates on the ball on his own, and you won't have to participate so much in the game. He will follow the ball on his own.

Tip

Try to get together a couple of "teams" of horse-and-rider pairs. Set up two goals in the riding arena, and play a game of ridden "soccer" with your horses. You will see how much fun this can be! Plus, it is also a good training exercise to improve horse and rider communication, as well as teaching the horse to accept large strange objects without fear.

1 It is fun to play "soccer" on horseback in teams of two.

2 Horses can get quite close to each other when playing ball, so be sure other riders and horses have been properly introduced to the ball and are behaved in close quarters.

Cooling Down ●●●

Just like with any good workout for human athletes, whether trained under saddle or in hand, the horse should be allowed to stretch and relax at the end. That doesn't mean that you stay in the arena, although a nice walk on a long rein around the perimeter of the ring can be lovely. Or you can dismount and walk a few rounds next to your horse—not only is that a nice change for him, it also loosens up tired rider muscles.

It is important that the horse is allowed to stretch and relax at the end of a work session. Every athlete deserves a proper cool down to avoid muscle problems.

WHAT IT LOOKS LIKE

Ride around the whole arena at the walk or trot on a long rein. Encourage your horse to drop his head and stretch forward and downward. This lifts his back and causes the horse to step farther under with his hind legs. Perfect!

If you are leading your horse from the ground, let the rope hang down long and walk a few times around the arena or out around your barn or pasture. Gradually your horse's head will drop, and he will not only have a nice stretch, but he find a place of quiet relaxation.

HOW TO DO IT

For correct stretching along the horse's topline and through-out his circle of muscles, it is important that his hind legs remain active, stepping well under his body. For that to occur when you're riding, you must continue to actively drive with your legs. Let the horse slowly "chew the reins out of your hands," reaching forward and downward into a soft inviting contact.

From the ground, gradually let the lead rope get longer and longer, and match your walk stride with your horse's. Let him drop his head. Don't let him wander, however.

"Good boy!" Praise is the most important motivator for the horse.

Tip

Toward the end of a training session, "give" your horse the reins now and then—give forward with your hands and lengthen the reins a bit. Don't take the reins back until your horse reaches for the contact in a relaxed stretch. Always praise him and leave him with friendly words.

Cleaning Up ●●●

Your horse has some free time ahead **and is excited to get back to the pasture. Unfortunately, you have a little more work to do! All the cones and poles have to be put away. If you ask really nicely, maybe your horse will help you!**

WHAT IT LOOKS LIKE

Admittedly, there is little the horse can do to help you with the poles, but sometimes you can actually get him to help with the cones. Many horses actually enjoy learning such simple tricks!

This works especially well with a horse that likes to put everything in his mouth. If they aren't leftover from your practice session, place three or four cones on the ground.

You can teach your horse to take the base of the cone in his mouth (watch that he

Romeo likes to help me pick up the cones.

He grabs a cone with his teeth and lifts it up.

Then he gives the cone to me and I take it.

His help makes cleanup much more fun!

doesn't bite through the plastic), lift it, and "hand" it to you.

HOW TO DO IT

Lead your horse to a cone and tip it over with your foot so your horse can easily grab and lift it by the bottom edge. If your horse isn't naturally "mouthy," you can rub some apple or something similar on the edge of the base in order to make grasping the cone "tasty."

Repeat with the other cones, giving a

verbal command to help cue the trick—for example, "Up!" If your horse nibbles around or near the cone, praise him immediately. You can give him a treat if you want. In this way, the horse learns quickly that you want him to mouth the cone. You can build on this initial behavior, rewarding his reaction to your command, until he finally learns to pick up the cone and give it to you. Praise him immediately.

Thank You ●●●

Have you praised your horse today? Horses are eager to learn when it is worth it to them. What makes it "worth it" to them differs from horse to horse and according to the situation. Sometimes a treat motivates, as does abundant petting, or just a quick word of praise in passing. Experiment with what the best, "Thank you," is for your horse. You can express praise in different ways.

A friendly, "Attaboy!" or "Good!" can be used frequently while riding without interrupting the exercise. Pay attention to the tone of your voice since that determines the horse's understanding of the word. A brief stroke on the neck while riding is also good and gives the horse instant feedback. This is important since praise must always immediately follow the good behavior for it to reinforce it. You can also show a horse that he has responded correctly to an aid by discontinuing the aid. Removal of pressure to which he responded tells him that he did something right. In this way your horse stays sensitive. Why should he respond to your leg pressure if the pressure from your leg never goes away?

Turnout with a friend is a wonderful reward after work is done.

1 Shir Khan loves to be petted.
2 Of course, a treat is even better!

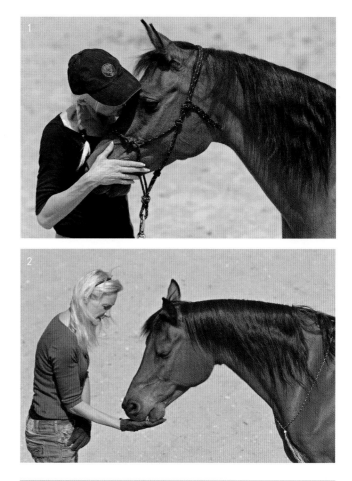

Breaks are important in all training sessions because they give the horse some time to think. Horses often start yawning during the rest periods—not because they are bored but because they are processing what they have learned.

Some horses also like to be taken care of or pampered a bit after they are untacked. They enjoy having the sweat washed off or a little massage. Others love to be allowed a roll or to be free to run in the pasture with a friend.

Notice your horse's mood after your next ride. What do you think he would like the most as a "thank you"?

Tip

You can't train a horse without well-timed praise. It isn't enough to give his neck a little scratch on your way back to the barn after the ride. Positive, desired behavior must always be rewarded as close to the time of the behavior as possible. Only then can the horse understand *why* he is being praised and be motivated to show the desired behavior again.

The Team

Here I am with my horses Shir Khan and Romeo.

Lena Throm

Silke Smeets

About Me

I have been riding for 40 years and have focused intensely on natural horsemanship, groundwork, and trick training. I teach lessons and clinics in Germany and elsewhere.

I have been very close to my two horses, Shir Khan and Romeo, for many years. Shir Khan is a very sensitive Russian Arab who can do many tricks with only a small hand signal from me. Romeo is a very talented horse under saddle. He learns quickly and likes to always be busy. I am often asked about his breed: He is a Weser-Ems German Riding Pony.

Lena Throm

Lena and Encantada are a true, all-around equestrian pair. Since she was born, the now 11-year-old Andalusian mare has accompa-nied Lena in all types of riding sports, including riding with the Garrocha (the pole used in bull fighting) and working equitation. Their focus, however, is classical dressage and performance.

Silke Smeets

Silke has been riding since childhood and is the owner of the Reimesheide Equestrian Center. She is an FN (sanctioned by the German national governing body for equestrian sports) trainer for competitive sports and competes successfully with her four dressage horses. She generously allowed us to do the photo shoot for this book at her facility, as well as making herself personally available as a riding model. She has a wonderful "feel" for horses.

Acknowledgments

• Thank you to riding instructor and horse trainer Silke Smeets (www.silke-smeets.de) for her support and expertise, and for allowing the use of her facility during the photo shoot for this book, as well as participating in the photos along with the horses Rondenjo, Ranjano, and Danubio.

• Thank you to my riding friend Lena Throm, along with her mare Encantada, for appearing in the photos in this book and being part of its creation despite a long trip and many other commitments. Encantada, an "all-around talent," was the perfect model for this book because she can demonstrate how these exercises are appropriate for all horses and all riders.

• Thank you to my horses Shir Khan and Romeo, for being motivated to participate in my exercises, as well as looking good while doing them.

• Thank you to Reitstall la Calma for providing the equipment for the photo shoot.

• Thank you to Kosmos Verlag and Birgit Bohnet, for always being open to new projects.

• Thank you to photographer Horst Stretferdt (www.foto-streitferdt.de) for his experience and knowledge of horses, which always enable him to get just the right shot.

Index